SHOPLIFTING IS STEALING!™

Why kids shoplift &
how to help them make better choices.

A guide for parents, teachers & communities.

By Judy Whalen

Shoplifting IS Stealing!™
Why kids shoplift & how to help them make better choices.
A guide for parents, teachers & communities.

Published by: It Starts With Us, Inc. ™
www.ItStartsWithUs.com
www.ShopliftingIsStealing.com

ISBN: 978-0615781815

Copyright 2013 by Judy Whalen and It Starts With Us, Inc.™. All rights reserved. Unless otherwise noted, no part of this book may be reproduced, stored in a retrieval system, transmitted in any form or by any means, electronic, mechanical photocopying, recording or transmitted in any form without express written permission from the author, except for brief quotations or critical reviews.

Disclaimer: The information and ideas in this book are for educational purposes only. Shoplifting is a serious problem that affects each individual differently. This book is not intended to be a substitute for consulting with an appropriate health care provider, family counselor, or legal counsel. The author and publisher disclaim any liability arising directly or indirectly from this book.

TABLE OF CONTENTS

Introduction *5*

"I Never Thought This Would Happen to My Daughter..." *9*

Shoplifting: A Hidden Crime *11*

The Facts *13*

What is Shoplifting? Who Shoplifts? *15*

Anatomy of a Crime *23*

The Reasons *25*

Serious Reasons for Concern *37*

More Reasons for Concern *43*

Signs the Your Child May Be Shoplifting *51*

How to Help Kids: Keys to Prevention and What to Do if Your Child Shoplifts *59*

Action Steps *73*

Other Tips for Parents: The Importance of Family *75*

Tips for Educators *83*

How to Get Your Community Involved *103*

Additional Resources *111*

About the Author *117*

INTRODUCTION

DO YOU KNOW WHERE YOUR CHILDREN ARE?

(Or more importantly ... Do you know what your children are doing?)

Many parents, educators, and community members understand the perils of drug and alcohol abuse, gang activity, and violence among youth. Yet, there exists a crime so commonplace, so insidious... that we rarely even consider it. In fact, some of us regularly commit this crime ourselves – at work, at school, or at the store. The crime? Shoplifting.

Shoplifting affects everyone – parents, children, communities, and businesses. This crime does not discriminate, as people of all ages, races, ethnicities and backgrounds shoplift every day. And it doesn't matter if a child or adult is wealthy, impoverished, highly educated, or academically-challenged, because there is no "typical" shoplifter; however, there are warning signs of shoplifting. Unfortunately, many people miss or ignore those signs – until it's too late.

But you don't have to feel helpless, frustrated, or misinformed. You can take action and help children make better choices today!

By reading this book, you'll learn important information about shoplifting, including:

• Shoplifting facts and statistics

• Reasons why people – especially children – shoplift

• The costs and consequences of shoplifting

• Signs that your child may be shoplifting

• Tips to prevent shoplifting

• Links to online shoplifting resources

For parents, this guide will present conversation starters to use with your child and offer ways to communicate more effectively with your son or daughter. Teachers reading this book will find valuable lesson plans, games, and role-playing situations to actively engage students with the topic of shoplifting. (Be sure to check out the ideas for partnering with local law enforcement and the list of suggested school-wide programs, clubs, and activities.) And for law enforcement officials and community members, we've provided a list of ways to partner with other businesses and community organizations in planning a *Shoplifting IS Stealing!*™ Community Awareness campaign.

Whether you're a teacher with a classroom full of students or a parent, this comprehensive guide will provide you with highly effective tools you need to prevent shoplifting and help kids make better decisions. Equipped with the suggested conversation starters, hypothetical situations and "talking points," you will increase both your confidence and effectiveness in discussing and dealing with shoplifting. And for those of you who are dealing with a child who has shoplifted, this book will address your concerns in a compassionate, supportive manner with practical advice and strategies that work.

As you read through this book remember, early intervention is the key to preventing shoplifting and juvenile crime and you can make a difference! After all, making a difference in our lives, families and communities starts with each one of us. If we want things to change, "It Starts With Us" so let's get started!

"I NEVER THOUGHT THIS WOULD HAPPEN TO MY DAUGHTER…"

Jane Smith (names have been changed) picked up the ringing phone, anticipating the call from her daughter Sarah. Her three friends had invited Sarah to spend the afternoon at the mall to catch a movie and do some window shopping. Jane had agreed to pick the girls up, and it was now 3 p.m., the time she had asked Sarah to check in. But the voice on the other end wasn't Sarah's. It was the voice of a police officer

"Is this Mrs. Jane Smith?"

Jane gripped the phone nervously. "Yes, it is. Who is this?" She proceeded to listen in shock and horror to Officer Williams. Apparently, Sarah and her friends were being held in custody by security at one of the mall's department stores. The reason? Shoplifting.

Jane tormented herself with questions on her short drive to the mall. Sarah? Shoplifting? Sarah was an honor student, involved with sports and community service projects. Jane had always felt fortunate that she was raising a "good girl" with responsible friends. But Jane's secure world was crumbling as she walked into the small room where the girls were being detained.

Sarah started crying as soon as Jane entered the room. "I'm so sorry, Mom!" she sobbed.

The only word Jane could muster was, "Why?"

Allison, one of Sarah's friends, spoke up. "It was just a CD! Sarah did it on a dare. It's all my fault, Mrs. Smith! I was the one who put her up to it. But it's not like we're criminals or anything! We didn't think it would be such a big deal."

The manager looked at each girl sternly. Then he spoke, disbelief and disgust apparent in his voice. "Just a CD? No big deal? I don't think you understand how serious shoplifting really is."

SHOPLIFTING: A HIDDEN CRIME

Jane never fathomed that her daughter would be apprehended for stealing. Many parents are no different. Though they may be aware that perils await their children as they approach the teenage years, many well-meaning parents may not feel comfortable or informed enough to discuss difficult topics with their children. Sadly, issues like sex, drugs, tobacco, and alcohol are conversations that numerous parents try to sidestep and avoid. The few parents who do initiate these discussions will, many times, inadvertently miss another all-important topic of conversation – shoplifting.

They may not fully understand how serious or rampant this crime is. Unfortunately, most parents won't grasp the repercussions of shoplifting until they receive a phone call similar to Jane Smith's.

THE FACTS

To give you a better idea of the scope of this problem, consider the following statistics:

- Shoplifting is the #1 property crime in the U.S.

- In the United States, there are more than 615,000 shoplifting incidents every day.[1]

- Losses due to retail theft totaled approximately $37.1 billion in 2010.[2]

- Approximately 23 million people (that's 1 in 11) shoplift; 6 million of these people are children and teens (ages 13-17).[3]

- Shoplifting costs retailers more than $25 million a day.[4]

- Shoplifting costs honest consumers about $300 per year in increased prices to cover the costs of this crime.

- Shoplifting is a gateway crime: 30% of prison inmates admit they started out as shoplifters.[5]

[1] Jack L. Hayes International, Inc.
[2] Source: University of Florida survey
[3] Source: National Crime Prevention Council
[4] Source: Rutgers Crime Prevention Service
[5] Source: *The Steal: A Cultural History of Shoplifting*, Rachel Shteir

The first section of this book provides information about chidren and shoplifting – who shoplifts, the underlying reasons someone steals, why shoplifting is a problem, the consequences of shoplifting, and how people get away with it. Then it equips you with the skills to identify the warning signs of shoplifting, a crucial element in prevention of this crime.

For those of you in the unfortunate situation of dealing with a child who has been caught shoplifting, the book shares with you numerous ways to handle the situation effectively, compassionately, and intelligently. Finally, it explores what we can do as teachers, parents, and law enforcement officials to take a proactive stance in preventing shoplifting.

It is my hope that this book will prepare you to not only discuss shoplifting with a child, but also to do your part in preventing that child from making a serious mistake that can result in regrettable consequences. Greater awareness regarding shoplifting is a vital first step, and from there we can work together as a community to nurture and encourage our children so that stealing is not an enticing choice for them. With a coordinated effort, we can work to significantly reduce the frequency of shoplifting and ultimately make our communities more vibrant and safer places to live and work.

WHAT IS SHOPLIFTING? WHO SHOPLIFTS?

The Cambridge dictionary defines shoplifting as "the illegal act of taking goods from a shop without paying for them." That means the person who shoplifts has not paid for the item and has no intention of doing so. Some people believe that shoplifting only occurs in retail stores, but that is an incorrect assumption: shoplifting can happen anywhere something is being sold, such as at open air markets, sporting events, school stores, etc.

Those who study this crime have found that two main types of shoplifters emerge. The first category is classified as "non-professional" shoplifters and often includes most kids and teens. This group of shoplifters may actually have the money to pay for the item, yet they find shoplifting fulfills emotional needs or gives the a sense of excitement. Others may steal things they really want, but don't have the money to pay for, and their shoplifting stems from addictions or materialistic desires. For these nonprofessional shoplifters, shoplifting allows them to acquire their "wants" without having to earn the funds to pay for the item(s). "Professionals" comprise the other major type of shoplifter. These thieves use stealing as a way to make a living, albeit illegally. They use shoplifting as a criminal enterprise – as a "business" and a way to meet their wants and needs.

Because people of every gender, age, race, social, and economic background shoplift, it is difficult to provide a simple composite sketch of the "typical" shoplifter. Terrence Shulman, a licensed social worker, certified addiction therapist, and founder for The Shulman Center for Compulsive Theft, Spending and Hoarding theorized in his book *Something for Nothing: Shoplifting and Recover* (2003) that most shoplifters fall into one of seven groups. These groups are: the professionals, the drug and gambling addicts, the impoverished, the thrill seekers, the absent-minded, the kleptomaniacs, and the addictive-compulsive shoplifters. Some shoplifters fall into more than one group either at the same time or over time. With Mr. Shulman's expressed permission, we have named these seven groups a bit differently:

• *The Cry-for-Help Shoplifter*

These shoplifters often have enough money in their pockets to pay for the items they stole. In addition, they know that shoplifting is wrong and expect to be punished if they're caught. Experts believe that these people (many times children and teens) are "acting out" by using the crime as a way to relieve stress or to make up for a loss in their lives. For example, kids whose parents are going through a divorce may consider the stolen items gifts to themselves during a trying time. Others may use stealing as a way to "get back" at someone, like a parent or friend, who has hurt him or her. And then there are other shoplifters in this category who steal because they are simply bored or depressed.

• *The Thrill-Seeking Shoplifter*

Thrill-seekers steal for excitement or on a dare. These individuals often steal in pairs or groups. Many children and teenagers who are acting on peer pressure fall into this category (see **The Reasons,** page 25, for more information on peer pressure). Thrill-seekers fin that their ability to get away with the crime provides them with an adrenaline rush. A thrill-seeking shoplifter who steals that first item easily may begin to find shoplifting an irresistible activity. Over time, thrill-seekers believe that what they have stolen is secondary to the feelings they get from shoplifting. That is, the sense of victory and excitement they achieve become the ultimate shoplifting prizes.[6]

---

[6] National Learning and Resource

• *The Substance-Abusing Shoplifter*

Substance abusers steal to pay for their addictive habits, such as drugs, alcohol or tobacco. Members of this group prefer to shoplift multiple items and often higher-end merchandise. They are usually less careful than professional thieves. These individuals are often found with drugs or drug paraphernalia in their possession upon apprehension. If they are caught, they will attempt to flee the scene and show little or no guilt if confronted.

• *The Impoverished Shoplifter*

These shoplifters steal out of economic need. Members of this group may exhibit poor hygiene and dress. In essence, they steal to survive. Typical shoplifting for them covers life's necessities, such as food, diapers, and toiletries. If they are caught, these people will express shame and remorse, but they will also reveal their frustrations concerning their lack of money. The impoverished group often blames others for their position in life.

• *The Kleptomaniac*

Members of this group steal for no reason other than compulsion. Often times, they steal items they don't even need or use. They have a mental illness and cannot stop themselves from stealing merchandise wherever they go. If a kleptomaniac is caught, that person will usually admit that he or she has an addiction to stealing. Kleptomaniacs often claim that they do not remember the act of shoplifting. They will also often say they don't know why they took an item in the first place.

• *The Absent-Minded Shoplifter*

Some people simply steal without being aware of it. This is most common in elderly people, by those on medications, or with people who are in a hurry. The next time you shop, notice how many stores require the cashier to ask the customer, "May I help you with any items in your cart?" This is a polite way of acknowledging that the shopper may forget to place all merchandise from the cart on the counter and become yet another absent-minded shoplifter. (Of course, it's a gentle reminder to those who may purposely "forget" to empty the cart or basket, too.)

This prompt helps to refocus a distracted consumer who may inadvertently walk off with unpaid merchandise due to legitimate inattentiveness. Another scenario of absent-minded shoplifting occurs when a small child picks up an item and walks out of the store without the parent's knowledge. Many times, the parent may be clueless about the theft until arriving at home (and the child shows Mom or Dad the candy, game, or toy).

If someone in this category is confronted, the individual typically expresses extreme remorse and will almost always pay for the item that person (or that person's child) accidentally picked up.

• *The Professional Shoplifter*

This group steals for profit or as a lifestyle. Professionals trea shoplifting as a career and a source of income. People in this group try to steal high-end or expensive items, and they often steal more than one item at a time. When they arrive at their shoplifting destination, they are prepared, often carrying tools to assist them. These individuals often resist arrest, usually by fleeing from th scene of the crime. However, if they are caught, they maintain composure and show no guilt, shame, or remorse for their actions.

KEY POINTS

- Shoplifters steal goods with no intention of paying for the items.

- People shoplift not only from retail establishments but also from places like open-air markets and school stores – basically, any where something is being sold.

- Shoplifters fall into two broad categories – professional and non-professional.

- There is no "typical" shoplifter, as people of any age, race, and background commit this crime.

- Seven shoplifting "groups" have been identified: cry-for-help shoplifters, thrill-seekers, substance-abusers, impoverished shoplifters, kleptomaniacs, absent-minded shoplifters, and professional shoplifters.

- Each type of shoplifter differs in his or her motivation for shoplifting. For example, kleptomaniacs steal to feed their compulsions, while thrill-seekers shoplift just to see how much they can get away with.

- The different shoplifter types will react in different ways if confronted. For instance, professional shoplifters rarely show remorse, while an absent-minded shoplifter will express guilt and offer to pay for the stolen item.

ANATOMY OF A CRIME

If you've ever wondered what shoplifters steal, and how they get away with their crimes, take a look at some information provided by the *Global Theft Barometer-Center for Retail Research – 2008 Report*. The items people most frequently shoplifted include:

1) Razor blades (Gillette)
2) Alcohol (branded spirits)
3) Toiletries, cosmetics and fine fragrance
4) Clothing and lingerie
5) Batteries (Duracell)
6) DVDs, CDs (rap and dance) and computer games
7) Pills, vitamins, contraceptives and pregnancy testers
8) Electric toothbrushes, Braun gas cylinders
9) Instant coffee
10) Steak and packs of meat

Another way shoplifters cheat businesses out of money is by cashing in on refunds they do not legitimately qualify for.

To steal items from a store, the criminals often remove identifying elements. They employ creative techniques to transport the items out of the store undetected. In fact, some people make an entire living off of shoplifting![7]

---

[7] Pepper Spray Store, as of Wednesday, 23-Nov-2011 02:57:43 CST

THE REASONS

Understanding *who* shoplifts is informative and important knowledge to have, but this information alone will not resolve the issue. It is also critical to understand the *reasons* why kids shoplift in the first place. However, just as it is difficult to narrow dow the description of shoplifter "types" into one definitive profile, it i equally challenging to provide a single reason *why* someone steals. Nevertheless, if we look at this crime in conjunction with what we know about the various types of shoplifters, we will gain a greater understanding of their reasoning.

Why Children and Teens Steal

For many parents, it can be challenging to understand what would motivate a child to shoplift. For this reason, examining the child's intention behind the crime merits its own discussion. In the majority of cases involving youth, peer pressure is the reason that drives many children to shoplift. Anyone familiar with kids understands that they have an overwhelming need and desire to belong. Children (teenagers especially) want to fit in with their peer group. So, if someone convinces them to steal something, they are quite susceptible to caving in to their friends' demands. In fact, according to the National Association for Shoplifting Prevention, 86% of children say they know someone who shoplifts, and 66% of these kids hang out with the shoplifters.

> *In the majority of cases involving youth, peer pressure is the reason that drives many children to shoplift.*

The pressure to steal may emerge with the desire to join a coveted clique – the "in" group. The child who aspires to associate with this group may view acceptance from the clique as a ticket to popularity, social recognition, and/or a feeling of belonging. Breaking the law may be worth it to the child, and he or she could be desperate enough to sacrifice good judgment and morals in exchange for ga ning access to an elite group.

Other children and teens who are thrill-seekers may begin shoplifting just to see if they can get away with it. They know what they are doing is wrong, but they think nothing will happen to them. Most shoplifters say the excitement they receive from "getting away with it" is an unbelievable high that is more rewarding than the merchandise they steal. Many times, their stealing is reinforced when they don't get caught. However, eventually they will get caught. The odds prove it. By then, the consequences may be severe.

As mentioned before, some children may shoplift in order to maintain a lifestyle they or their parents cannot afford (or that their parents refuse to buy for them). With shoplifting, these kids find they can wear the cool clothes and newest jewelry, possess the high-end cosmetics, and obtain the latest in sporting gear. Many times, they possess poor impulse control, which means that if they see something they want, they believe they need it now, and they will get it by any means possible – even if it means breaking the law.

The home environment is another critical element with respect to shoplifting. If a child feels neglected by family members, he or she may turn to shoplifting as a way of getting attention. Sometimes, the child will steal as an escape mechanism or a way to avoid thinking about family issues. Children who feel that their lives are out of control may use stealing as a means to gain a sense of power that they lack in other areas of their lives.

> *"If a child feels neglected by family members, he or she may turn to shoplifting as a way of getting attention."*

Other emotional factors may contribute to shoplifting, too. If a child suffers from depression, boredom, or anxiety, he or she may be at risk for engaging in risky behaviors like shoplifting. Similar to children with problems in the home, a child who experiences anxiety at school or work may shoplift to ease or avoid those nervous feelings. Insecure children who feel unworthy or unattractive may begin shoplifting as a way to increase self-worth through the false perception of power that shoplifting provides.

Unfortunately, another reason children steal is due to their addiction to drugs or alcohol. For an addict, priorities shift: the commitment to schoolwork, sports, and family will diminish for the person caught in the grip of addiction. If stealing is necessary to enable the person to get drunk or high, then in the addict's mind, the end justifies the means

Yet other children may shoplift because of a mental health disorder, such as kleptomania. Kleptomania is a condition that causes the person to steal compulsively. In other words, the intention of the thief is to feed the compulsion, and this ritual (stealing) provides relief for the person suffering from the disease.

Perhaps the most dangerous reason children choose to shoplift arise from the influences of a gang. Gang members will often require new recruits to steal as an initiation rite. Children who feel left out may relish the opportunity to feel wanted, and if the price for that acceptance is stealing, they are more than willing to oblige.

> **" Perhaps the most dangerous reason children choose to shoplift arise from the influences of a gang. "**

Children who shoplift but do not fit into any of the other "groups" essentially have difficulty distinguishing between right and wrong. For these children, they do not necessarily see anything amiss with what they are doing.

More About Kleptomaniacs and Why They Steal

Although many people believe that stealing is a personal choice, there are thousands of people worldwide who feel their lives of crime are out of their control. Individuals can become addicted to shoplifting in the same way that others become addicted to drugs, alcohol, gambling, or sex.

As previously mentioned, kleptomania is the recurring failure to resist the impulse to steal objects that are not personally needed. Although some view this disease as a rare condition, more and more people are being categorized as "stealing" addicts every year.

In one of his studies on shoplifting, psychologist Will Cupchik stated that most kleptomaniacs are otherwise law-abiding people who are looking to replace voids in their lives. Adults and kids can become addicted to shoplifting as a way to comfort themselves. In other words, kleptomaniacs often use the thrill they get from stealing as a way to deal with stressful or traumatic events in their lives that they are not otherwise equipped to handle. A unique aspect of this disease is that, instead of feeling guilty after committing a theft, those who are addicted to shoplifting experience feelings of relief; the criminal activity allows them an escape from the problems in their lives, and they find they cannot achieve this release without stealing.

In addition to the emotional payoffs, most kleptomaniacs also say they are drawn to the idea of getting something for nothing, no matter what that something is. In these cases, people often steal items they don't need or can't even use, such as clothes that don't fit. As with any addiction, the first step an individual suffering from kleptomania must take towards recovery is admitting that he or she has a problem and wants help to overcome it. Treatments for kleptomania include therapy, medication, and support groups. Kleptomania is a serious condition that requires professional treatment.

A Closer Look at Shoplifters with Addictive/Compulsive Personalities

75% of all shoplifters fall into this group. Characteristics often include repressed anger and signs of other compulsive behaviors, such as substance abuse, overeating, etc. Adults and kids with addictive tendencies often do not care about obtaining things for themselves so they will steal inexpensive items to give away as gifts. These people will exhibit overwhelming guilt and shame if they are caught; they may even cry when confronted. Unfortunately, it's easy for shoplifting to become addictive. A person who shoplifts experiences a "high," or surge of adrenaline, and some of this can be attributed to "getting away with" the crime. This is not unlike the high that drug addicts or alcoholics feel. This temporary rush serves to relieve feelings of depression or stress, so the person continues the destructive behavior, even though he or she may wish to stop. As mentioned above, kleptomaniacs are particularly sensitive to these feelings.

Why Celebrities Shoplift

We have all read newspaper stories and seen television shows about celebrities and other prominent individuals who shoplift.

Why would people who are wealthy and famous steal? To many of us this seems absurd and ridiculous. However, there are various reasons these privileged people decide to steal.

Like many other shoplifters, celebrities often steal for the thrill of it. In other words, experimenting with what they can get away with becomes a challenge or game. Famous shoplifters steal out of want, not need. Some of them lack basic moral values and don't see anything wrong with stealing something whether they need it or not.

Over time, celebrities who shoplift could fall victim to the belief that, because they are famous, they are invincible. Therefore, they believe they won't have to suffer the consequences that other people face if they're caught. And those who are caught may not mind the scandal. Celebrities who relish the press in this type of situation subscribe to the philosophy that any publicity is good publicity. In this way, getting arrested can become an effective, albeit dysfunctional, way to boost their careers.

Prominent people don't just shoplift to promote themselves. Many steal for the same reasons other people do (addictions, negative feelings, the wish to escape, the desire for power, etc.). All of these are tempting reasons to steal, and the celebrity may find that the act of shoplifting fills certain voids in their lives

It is important to remind kids that even though they may look up to celebrities, famous people can make poor choices just like anyone else. They merely have the misfortune to have their mistakes publicized every day for the world to witness. Teachers, parents, and concerned citizens can use these public scandals to teach our youth that no matter who the person is; there are consequences for one's actions. Visit www.ShopliftingIsStealing.com to read more about how to keep our children from ending up in the public eye.

KEYPOINTS

- Just as there are many different types of shoplifters, there are numerous reasons why people shoplift.

- Emotional issues in children may lead them to shoplift.

- Peer pressure can motivate a child to shoplift.

- Children with thrill-seeking tendencies may begin shoplifting as a way to experience an adrenaline rush.

- Children with issues at home may shoplift as a means of acting out, gaining a sense of control, or as an escape mechanism.

- Some children shoplift because they have not learned to distinguish right from wrong.

- Some children shoplift to support a more luxurious lifestyle of designer labels and the latest electronics.

- Some peer pressure comes from dangerous gang influences, while other children experience the pressure of wanting to fit into a particular group or clique.

- People with addictive-compulsive personalities may use shoplifting as a way to act upon their compulsions and find their stealing addictive.

- Celebrities shoplift for many of the same reasons everyday people do: thrill-seeking, a lack of morals, addictions, other emotional issues, etc.

- Some celebrities relish the publicity they receive after being caught from shoplifting.

- Drug addicts will steal in order to obtain money for drugs to support their harmful habit.

- Kleptomaniacs steal because they cannot help themselves.

SERIOUS REASONS FOR CONCERN

As mentioned before, shoplifting is often overlooked as a serious problem. Parents and educators may not know the consequences when discussing shoplifting with kids. Law enforcement officers may be preoccupied with a large volume of more serious crimes. Retail merchants may be concerned that prosecuting shoplifters will cause ramifications for their business. So, why should you be concerned if your child (or a child you know) shoplifts?

Shoplifting is a Gateway Crime That Can Lead to More Serious Crime

Is there a correlation between offenders who shoplift and the use of drugs or involvement in other types of crime? Many parents fear that shoplifting will lead to other illegal activities, such as drugs, drinking, truancy, and burglary. Is this fear legitimate? According to the research, the answer is yes, so please don't be fooled into thinking that shoplifting is an inconsequential passing childhood phase.

Researchers have found that 55% of adult shoplifters started shoplifting in their teens[8] Clearly, shoplifting can become a lifelong problem. The correlation between shoplifting and other crimes is unmistakable, as 30% of prison inmates started their lives of crime as shoplifters.[9] Children between the ages of 12 and 17 who shoplifted are five times more likely to be involved with other crimes at some point. [10]

> **" *Researchers have found that 55% of adult shoplifters started shoplifting in their teens.* "**

These children may be involved in other risky behaviors or crimes including drugs, drinking at least once a week, and truancy from school. Just as experimentation with certain drugs opens the door for more serious drug abuse, shoplifting items and getting away with it leads to more shoplifting and other crimes that may be even more violent and dangerous. If the child or teen is a repeat offender, the risks increase: repeat shoplifting offenders are much more likely to be involved with other illegal activities than those who have never shoplifted. For males (ages 18-30), those who have

---

[8] Sources: National Association for Shoplifting Prevention; *Why Do Shoplifters Steal?* by Peter Berlin; USA Weekend, October 16-18, 1998; Today's Coverage, May 26, 1998; *Retail Theft Trends Report: A Snapshot of Shoplifting in America,* by Read Hayes, 1998.
[9] Parent Tip Booklet (from ShopliftingIsStealing.com), p. 3
[10] Parent Tip Booklet (from ShopliftingIsStealing.com), p. 10

shoplifted in the past year are two times more likely to be involved with other crimes. Worse yet, females in this same age group are three times as likely to be involved with other illegal activities.[11]

A Child's Post-Secondary Education and Future Employment Are at Stake

Some universities and colleges do background checks on prospective students. At times, a college or university might ask if the applicant has a criminal record. If the record has been expunged, the prospective student can claim that he or she does NOT have a criminal record. Gone are the days of the attitude that everything a child does somehow "disappears" when he or she turns 18. Juvenile records are no longer wiped clean in most states.[12] In fact, the person with the record must request that his or her record be expunged when that person turns 18.[13]

If the child shoplifts on campus during the college years, he or she may face not only criminal charges but also disciplinary consequences from the college or university. Finally, when a child graduates and enters the workforce, many employers do background checks

---

[11] Parent Tip Booklet (from ShopliftingIsStealing.com), p. 10

[12] Family Circle, June 2011

[13] *from* girlshealth.gov, "Your Future"

on employees prior to hiring. Though employers do not have access to juvenile records, a shoplifting offense by an 18-year-old will show up on a criminal record, as that teen is now considered an "adult". It is important that parents understand the laws of their municipality and state. Some states will process a 16 or 17-year-old through the adult court system.

Consequences for Shoplifting are Steep

If a person is convicted of shoplifting, he or she may be ordered to pay fines, make restitution, perform community service, be placed on probation or be sentenced to serve time in a detention facility or juvenile hall. Fine amounts vary by state and municipality (and depend upon the shoplifting circumstances.) Fines can be as high as $10,000! Parents are responsible for payment if their child is not able to pay. In addition to the monetary consequences, think about how a possible incarceration would affect your son or daughter. Imagine your child being led out of a store in handcuffs or spending time in a holding cell at the local police department or being sentenced to time in a youth detention center. Do you want your child to have that kind of life experience in their formative years?

Even though shoplifters face severe consequences, there is evidence that shoplifting is on the rise. According to a summary of *The*

Ethics of American Youth (The Josephson Institute of Ethics), one in three boys and one in four girls admitted to stealing from a store in 2008. This increased from 28% to 30% between 2006 and 2008.

> *" One in three boys and one in four girls admitted to stealing. "*

With more children shoplifting than ever before, it is imperative that you educate your child on how to handle a shoplifting situation (or the pressure from friends to shoplift). The chances of your child being exposed to this type of crime is becoming a greater probability, and waiting until shoplifting occurs can be a costly option.

These troubling statistics prove that preventative action and education at an early age will help lower the number of shoplifters. Do you want your child to become another statistic for America to analyze?

KEY POINTS

- Shoplifting is considered a gateway crime to other criminal activity.

- Those who shoplift as children may turn to drugs, alcohol, and more frequent shoplifting.

- Repeat shoplifting offenders are more likely to turn to other forms of criminal activity than someone who has only shoplifted once.

- Females who shoplift are more likely to become involved with other crimes than males.

- A child who shoplifts puts his educational future in jeopardy be cause colleges and universities may be reluctant to admit a student with a criminal record.

- Employers who are aware of a job seeker's criminal history – especially when the history includes shoplifting – may refuse to hire that person, especially if the job requires the handling of money.

- Steep fin s, restitution, community service, and jail time are just a few of the consequences of shoplifting.

MORE SERIOUS CONCERNS...

For Merchants

Shoplifting affects everyone in our society, including businesses, as U.S. businesses lose an average of $25 million a day due to shoplifting. For every dollar recovered from shoplifting, $37 is lost.[14] Think of it this way: when a store experiences high shoplifting rates, the business will need to take measures to prevent such crimes from occurring frequently. These measures can include implementing a bag-check policy, installing security cameras and/or alarms, and hiring security guards. All of these measures can be quite expensive. When merchants catch shoplifters in the act, they can, fortunately, recover stolen merchandise. However, the costs of apprehending and prosecuting offenders can be quite high. This places even more expenses on the merchant and ends up increasing prices paid by honest consumers.

Shoplifters aren't always customers. Sometimes shoplifters are employees. One out of every 30 employees was apprehended for theft from his/her employer in 2008 (based on comparison data of

---

[14] Jack Hayes International, Inc.

over 2.1 million employees).[15] Rates of employee theft vary by store type, as convenience stores have the highest rate of employee theft, and furniture stores have the lowest rates.

Some employers have taken measures to prevent workplace shoplifting, including improved inventory systems, clear expectations, and a system of checks and balances. Software and surveillance systems that monitor inventory and employee activity can quickly spot unusual dips in inventory and instances of "sweethearting" – the act of pretending to scan an item for sale but (in reality) not swiping the item – or merely ringing it up improperly – and simply giving it away to friends and family. Certainly, these technological aids can help employers a great deal.

Besides using technology, other employers make it abundantly clear that shoplifting will not be tolerated, and they take time to clarify the consequences of this offense with their workers. Many times, this communication results in reduced shoplifting among staff in a business.

Finally, having several people in positions to oversee finances prevents one person from monopolizing access to bookkeeping and

---

[15] Jack Hayes International, Inc.

cash flow. It is not only a safeguard against embezzlement, but also provides multiple "eyes" on the books to detect and report any suspicious activity.

Unfortunately for the merchants, these valuable resources cost time and money.

When the operating costs increase as a result of shoplifting prevention measures, it forces business owners to raise their prices to make up for losses incurred from shoplifters. As a result of higher prices, businesses may begin to lose customers, even loyal ones. People will begin to take their business elsewhere if they find they can obtain the same items at another store for a lower cost. Eventually, this may lead a merchant to go out of business. In fact, one out of every three new businesses fails (in part) due to the losses incurred from shoplifting.[16]

Finally, shoplifting puts a stigma on teenagers who are old enough to be shopping without adult supervision. Since teens are often seen as the largest shoplifting threat – and they do make up 25% of convicted shoplifters – business owners often feel that they must discourage them from shopping in their stores. This leads to

[16] Jack Hayes International, Inc.

the loss of potential business from teen shoppers who may legitimately want to patronize a particular store. For those who merely want to shop, being discriminated against by merchants can be irritating or upsetting.

It is possible to teach children that honest consumers, the merchant, and the community as a whole lose when even one person shoplifts. Using the tools *Shoplifting IS Stealing!*™ provides and working with local law enforcement and merchants can help prevent kids from becoming another statistic. Please visit our website www.ShopliftingIsStealing.com to find out how we can take action together to prevent the gateway crime of shoplifting from spiraling out of control and leading kids to lives of crime.

Impact on the Consumer

Shoplifting doesn't only affect store owners' bottom lines, it affects consumers as well. Even if you and your family are honest, law-abiding consumers, your pocketbook is affected by this crime. The costs related to shoplifting are absorbed not only by merchants but also by you, the consumer. You will find yourself paying higher prices to cover the costs of stolen merchandise, loss prevention, etc. The average family pays merchants an extra $400 to $500 a year for shoplifting-related expenses.[17]

---

[17] Jack Hayes International, Inc.

When a merchant takes measures to prevent shoplifting, it results in a variety of inconveniences which make shopping cumbersome and difficult. Instead of being able to simply enter a store and browse, you could be subjected to security alarms or guards at the store entrance. If you are shopping for clothes and choose to go into a fitting room, you might have to check your bags with the dressing room attendant. And don't forget about the cumbersome security devices attached to products like perfume, electronics, and clothing. Clothing can be difficult to try on with security devices positioned in uncomfortable places, and items you want to purchase could be locked up. This means that you need to find an employee who can unlock the case or open the shoplift-proof packaging to allow you to make your purchase.

If shoplifting expenses drive merchant prices too high or force stores out of business, it is possible that your favorite stores will no longer exist, and you may be forced to travel further to find alternative suppliers. When businesses limit the variety of items they offer because of the revenue loss due to shoplifting, it is quite possible that you will need to shop in multiple places to buy things that you previously could purchase in the same store. Indeed, shoplifting affects everyone in society.

KEY POINTS

- Businesses lose millions of dollars a day from shoplifting.

- Merchants who experience frequent shoplifting may be forced to implement heightened security measures.

- Even when a merchant recovers stolen merchandise, the cost involved for prosecuting the offender places additional costs on the business owner.

- Businesses who fall victim to shoplifting may be forced to increase their prices.

- Higher prices may result in lost business, as customers will turn to other merchants who sell the same item at a lower price.

- With increased incidents of shoplifting, teenagers become stigmatized because this age group represents a large percentage of shoplifters.

- Business owners may ban teens from stores – even the law-abiding ones who legitimately want to shop.

- Honest customers absorb the costs of shoplifting by paying higher prices for certain goods.

- New security measures create inconveniences for the shopper, such as cumbersome security tags and packaging, metal detectors, and bag-checks.

- A customer's favorite store may be forced out of business if the operating expenses from shoplifting become too great.

- Shoppers may need to travel further to find similar goods when shoplifting-ravaged stores go out of business.

SIGNS THAT YOUR CHILD MAY BE SHOPLIFTING

It is important to determine the cause of the problem in order to solve shoplifting and prevent it from happening again. Taking an active role in your child's life could save him or her from making this mistake in the first place – or from making it again if she or he has already shoplifted.

Listening to your child's problems, concerns, and feelings on the issue of stealing is the key. We will address ways to work with your child in a proactive way in the next section, but first it is imperative to know the signs to look for that indicate your child may be involved with shoplifting.

What to Look For

Do you know what signs or behaviors may indicate that your child (or your child's friend) is shoplifting? There is no profile of a typical shoplifter because, as mentioned earlier, shoplifters come from all ages, ethnicities, backgrounds, and income levels. However, there are some general behaviors that should raise red flags. Below are signals to watch for so that you can take appropriate action.

Your child has a sudden change in attitude or persona, especially around family members

This can include anything from becoming increasingly isolated or secretive to becoming rebellious and argumentative. In the past, parents have associated these changes as a sign of depression, suicidal tendencies, or drug use. While these indicators could be linked to those factors, be aware that such changes in your child may also be a sign of shoplifting.

Your child exhibits an overall change in behavior

New behavior might include staying out past curfew, sneaking out after hours, lying, and other forms of dishonesty. Children sometimes become more secretive as well – about their money, new clothes, new equipment, etc. If your child suddenly isolates himself from others in the family and family activities, shoplifting is one possible explanation for this new behavior. Children who shoplift may become more argumentative, defensive and less cooperative, too.

Clearly, it is difficult at times to know when changes are due to puberty, hormones, or normal "growing pains", but any time your child changes and that change is incredibly sudden, you need to be on red alert that this may not just be the sign of normal developmental phases. Many parents realize in hindsight that the signs were there, and they simply ignored their gut feelings. For this reason, learn to listen to your instincts when you feel something has gone off-track with your child.

Your child suddenly has new personal belongings, the source of which is unknown

Any expensive items (CDs, DVD, electronic equipment, games, etc.) you find – but don't know where they came from – should raise concern. Realize that your child may claim the item is a "gift" from a friend to avoid suspicion. Of course, it's difficult for a parent to think his or her child is lying, but once again, sudden new possessions are warning signs. Another indication of stealing is that your child is giving expensive gifts to family or friends – gifts far greater in value than your child's income from a job or allowance. An abrupt change in physical appearance is another cause for concern. If you start to notice new and/or expensive clothing your child is wearing that you didn't purchase, it may be time to investigate to find out where and how your child obtained these items.

Your child possesses large amounts of money from unknown sources

This includes large amounts of money that are not from you, a gift from someone else, or earned by your child from a job. Of course, it is valuable for children to learn to manage their own money, whether that comes from an allowance or part-time job. And it is equally vital that children have some input and a certain degree of control over their finances. However, if you are aware of how much, realistically, your child earns, you will be in a better position to recognize if the amount of spending money suddenly exceeds his or her honest earnings.

You see changes in your child's academic work

Significant changes may include any of the following: a drop in grades, less interest in school, loss of interest in extracurricular activities, lack of motivation, etc. Sometimes a move to a new school, changing from elementary to middle school (or middle school to high school) is the culprit when grades fall. Other times, social issues can get in the way of learning; a child who is having problems with friends or with bullying may find it difficult to focu in class. These are typical reasons why grades may decline for a student, especially if this drop occurs suddenly. Once again, remember that this is also a possible sign of shoplifting.

Your child suddenly changes friends or groups of friends

Most children say they shoplift because of peer pressure. Most kids just want to fit in and be accepted, but it is especially important to be concerned if these new friends appear to be a negative influenc on your child. Fortunately, some children may cultivate new friendships because they gravitate towards strong, healthy relationships. On the flip side, a sudden change in peer group may indicate something more serious.

Experts recommend that parents get to know their children's friends. As children become more independent, this becomes increasingly difficult. It's all too easy for older children and teens to meet up with friends, ride a bike to the neighbor's, drive to someone else's house, etc. It is not uncommon, as children get older, for parents to find that their children have friends they've never even met! If you get to know your child's peer group, though, you can become attuned to behaviors and attitudes among their friends that may be influencing your child negatively, including rule-breaking and lying.

Your child is fired from a job for unknown and/o suspicious reasons

If your child works at a part-time job where he or she handles money or merchandise and is suddenly let go, investigate! Unfortunately, it might not be a clash of personality with the manager or downsizing (even if your child says this is the case). If the firing happens suddenly, this is another red flag Employers whose workers turn in cash register receipts that are consistently short or notice that their merchandise tends to go missing during your child's shift will not tolerate these "mistakes" for long. The best way to know if our children are making the right decisions is to pay attention to what they do. The more we know, the better we are able to give to our children the tools they need to help them make those decisions.

Shoplifting is one of those activities that may be difficult to detect. It is not limited to troubled children or teens with social, emotional, or behavioral issues. Many "model" youth who do their homework, get good grades, act responsibly, and help out around the house can have a problem with shoplifting. So, while shoplifting can be the behavioral manifestation that results from a child's problems, shoplifting can also happen among children who are normal, well-adjusted kids. [18]

---

[18] Source: Alexa Thomson (fgcu) facts-about-shoplifting

KEY POINTS

- As a parent, it is important to know the signs that indicate a child may be involved with shoplifting.

- Sudden changes in personality may be a sign that your child is shoplifting.

- A child who shoplifts may suddenly change his or her behavior. For example, he or she may become increasingly dishonest, isolated, or secretive.

- When your child suddenly possesses new personal belongings and you don't know how or where the item(s) came from, it may mean that your child has begun shoplifting.

- Large amounts of money from unknown sources may be another cause for concern. Even if a child has a job, shoplifting could be a factor if the amount of money clearly surpasses his or her normal income level.

- Another sign of shoplifting is a downward trend in schoolwork and general loss of interest in activities your son or daughter once enjoyed.

- If your child suddenly changes friends, be aware that shoplifting is one possible reason for this shift.

- Children who are suddenly fired from a job with unknown reasons may have been suspected or guilty of shoplifting.

HOW TO HELP KIDS: KEYS TO PREVENTION AND WHAT TO DO IF YOUR CHILD SHOPLIFTS

For parents...

Parents who are concerned that their child might be shoplifting may not know how to approach the situation, and even those parents who are already aware that their child has shoplifted may struggle with how to handle the issue. Below are a few tips for addressing the issue of shoplifting with your child, whether (1) your child has actually been accused of shoplifting; (2) you merely have your suspicions; or (3) you want to formulate a plan to take preventative measures so your child does not shoplift.

Take action immediately

The longer you wait, the greater the problem can become. Talking to your child is the logical first step, even if you are afraid of the a -

swers you may receive from your child. Most children will respond best if they feel that you have approached them in a caring, non-threatening way. Let your child know that you are speaking to him or her out of love and concern. Many parents meet with the greatest success if they refrain from criticizing, as many children will shut out parents if they feel they are being "attacked" or interrogated.

Emphasize that the truth is more important to you than the information that is revealed, no matter how embarrassing, shocking, or painful it may be to you or your child. A great way to encourage this is to keep communication with your child open and honest. Describe the changes in attitude, behavior, appearance, etc. that you are noticing and try to express your concerns reasonably. Kids will be more likely to listen and be receptive to your message if you discuss the problem with them rather than lecturing them. On the other hand, if your child fears your reaction, he or she may refuse to tell you the truth, no matter how much evidence you may have to support your suspicions.

Obviously, open communication is best when it has been established through the years, but it's never too late to start! If you feel that your child isn't comfortable sharing this information with you, you may wish to find a family member or friend that your child may be more inclined to talk to. With this third party present, the three of you can work together to not only support your child but also effectively deal with whatever issues arise.

While being proactive is essential, it's equally important not to jump to conclusions. If you've ever heard about hypochondriasis in medical students (where prospective doctors think they've contracted every disease or ailment they learn about in medical school), it is just as easy to suspect that every change in your child is the result of criminal or illegal activity. Temper the rush to judgment and balance it with involved awareness in your child's life, and you will be in a better position to know when to take action and when to be patient.

Knowledge is power. Talk to the other adults in your child's life (teachers, parents of friends, etc.), and try to get the facts about your child and his or her friends. It may help to obtain opinions from someone outside of your immediate family. Sometimes a friend's parents or teachers hold a separate piece of a larger puzzle, and when those seemingly disparate parcels of information come together, a full picture emerges. The information gleaned from various sources may allay your fears if you realize there is a harmless, logical explanation for the questionable behavior. In other instances, the new information may further reinforce your suspicions, in which case immediate action may be required on your part. This has been mentioned before, but it bears repeating: a terrific way to know your child better is by getting to know your child's friends. The only way you'll know what's going on in your child's life is to connect with his or her peers and their parents on a deeper level. This is also a way for you to use your instincts to decide if a particular friend or group of friends is a good personality match and influence on your child.

Of course, it's impossible to completely control whom your child associates with (and becoming too overbearing in this area may backfire, causing your child to purposely hang out with "bad" kids, just to spite you!); yet you can rely on your better judgment when deciding which friends visit your house regularly, where you allow your child to go, and which activities you allow your child to participate in.

When you have reservations about certain friends, you can use that knowledge to steer your child in more desirable directions. Consider making positive friends and activities easily-accessible for your son or daughter so that the negative relationships begin to fade. Yes, this will take time and effort on your part as a parent.

And yes, there is a fine line that exists between encouraging certain friendships and forcing them. However, the benefits of your dil - gence and hard work can pay huge dividends when you find that your child spends most of his or her time engaged in healthy pursuits with positive people.

Be clear about your standards and family values

Don't assume your child can read your mind! Be sure your son or daughter knows your family's values, understands that stealing is wrong, and knows that there are serious consequences for those who to shoplift (or continue to shoplift after being caught repeatedly for shoplifting). Conveying this message is not a one-shot deal, either. You will find it most effective if you embed this message into conversation after conversation over the years. Children thrive on repetition. Discussing your family's values and the moral implications of shoplifting is one of those topics that need continual reiteration. Also, be aware that children learn the most from example. You have to model the behavior you expect from your child. Tasting grapes at the grocery store could be considered shoplifting, so please think about your behavior as well as talking to your children about theirs.

In your conversations, explain to your child that adhering to basic ethical standards can lead to a bright, promising future. Living a life of integrity is important as a child, teen and adult. Again, kids learn most from observing adult behavior. Examine your own habits as you discuss shoplifting with your child.

Another helpful hint is to take the time to ask your child about his or her value system. Ask "what if" questions to see what your child would do in certain situations. For example, you can ask, "What would you do if one of your friends took a candy bar from the convenience store, and you knew about it?" (See the "Action Step" at the end of this chapter for more examples of "what if" questions). This will help you understand your child's thought processes and level of maturity and moral reasoning. It's also a great springboard for further conversation where you can share your own opinions about shoplifting.

> *Take the time to ask your child about his or her value system.*

Teach your child what to do if she or he feels pressured to shoplift. Discuss your feelings about shoplifting and what you would do if she or he got into a bad situation. Make sure your child knows all the options and help them choose the best one.

If you feel comfortable, role play various scenarios with your child. This will allow your son or daughter to feel prepared with ideas of what to say and do in a high-pressure situation. The more he or she rehearses responses, the easier it will be for your child to do the right thing, even when peer pressures mount.

Keep tabs on your child

Know where your child is at all times. One way to do this is to make it clear that when they are not at home, they need to communicate where they are, whom they are with, and when they will be home. Without being overly paranoid, you can occasionally check up on your child to ensure that he or she has told you the truth concerning his or her whereabouts. If your child consistently displays responsibility and dependability in this area, you may wish to reward the behavior with increased freedoms (within reason, of course). If, however, you find your child takes advantage of the freedoms or lies with respect to his or her whereabouts, setting limits and establishing reasonable consequences for dishonesty and irresponsibility will reinforce your values. Most children want to be treated as mature individuals. When they make the connection that there's a direct correlation between their level of personal integrity and the freedoms that are granted to them, they are more motivated to earn your trust and respect.

Encourage your child to invite their friends to spend time at your home. One way to do this is to stock the house with snacks and drinks: many kids will go anywhere that food is offered! Having your child's friends over is a wonderful way to learn more about your child and your child's friends while keeping an eye on your son or daughter.

Experts advise supervising your child, even during the teenage years. This means making sure you are still aware of his or her activities and being at home with your child as much as you can. Of course, the more independent your child becomes, the more comfortable you can be in giving your child more freedom, including time at home alone. Just keep in mind that teenagers who are unsupervised are more likely to be shoplifters. This is directly related to the number of evenings they are allowed to go out on their own. Once again, if your child is unsupervised for a period of time, do your best to keep that timeframe small. The fewer unsupervised hours your child has, the less chance he or she has of giving in to any temptations or peer influences.

At what point is a parent hovering too much? When is a parent being too permissive? Many parents find that what works for one family may not succeed with another: some children may need more supervision, while others need less. With this in mind, understand that it may take some time for you to strike that balance that works best for your family's needs and schedules.

When your child is at another friend's house, consider checking to be sure that there is adequate supervision there. A quick call to the friend's home can verify (or contradict) the story your child has told you. As much as we would like to believe that the parent is home – especially if the child claims adults are in the house – there are times when children will lie. They may reason that if you knew there was no supervision, your answer would be "no". Rather than be left out of a get-together or activity, your child may be dishonest with you in order to spend time with friends.

As in other situations, be clear that honest, responsible communication and behavior will be rewarded, and if you find that your child has not been forthcoming in these areas, you may need to limit your child's freedoms for a time. Most important is for your son or daughter to realize that privileges can be earned back with consistent honest behavior in the future. Not surprisingly, if your child feels that he or she is on restriction "for life," the motivation to do the right thing may wane.

> **Some children may need more supervision, while others need less.**

My Child Was Caught Shoplifting: Now What?

If you find yourself in the difficult position of learning that you child has been caught and/or convicted for shoplifting, you may be experiencing strong emotions – anger, sadness, confusion. These are normal feelings to experience in this kind of situation. Luckily, there are simple steps you can take to deal with the crisis effectively. Now more than ever, you will need to both maintain your composure and also be there to support your child to get through the initial fall-out from the crime. After the incident, it is equally important to continue to provide a consistent support structure so your child learns healthier behaviors, forges new friendships (if this was a contributing factor), and knows that – even though you have been let down by these poor choices – you still love your child and are there for him or her.

First, cooperating with law enforcement officials will benefi everyone in the long run. While most parents hate to see their children suffer, you also need to let your child know in no uncertain terms that you do not approve of the behavior. If you make excuses or do everything in your power to smooth things over and prevent your child from experiencing any discomfort for his or her actions, you may temporarily avoid drama and distress for your child. Unfortunately, making all of your child's problems "go away" is more of a disservice to the child than a help, as he or she may not learn a lesson this time and may be compelled to continue the illegal behavior because it seemed like "no big deal".

Next, if the shoplifting occurred in a group, work with the friends' parents to form a unified front. Hopefully, you can support each other during a trying time and be there for each other to vent your own fears and frustrations as a parent. Obviously, if the friends' parents are trying to cover up for the children's crimes, this may not be an option, but it is worth investigating to gauge the other parents' reactions.

Finally, if shoplifting continues to be a problem, you may need to seek professional help. Don't feel as if you need to shoulder this burden alone. There are many qualified professionals that can help you and your child navigate these issues. Other emotional factors may be at work, and getting to the root causes will be necessary in ending the unwanted behaviors.

Prevention is the greatest lesson a parent can teach their children. Visit our website www.ShopliftingIsStealing.com for guidance as you go through challenges with shoplifting.

KEY POINTS

- If you know your child is shoplifting or you suspect shoplifting activity, take action immediately.

- Cultivate open and honest communication with your child so that he or she feels comfortable coming to you to discuss important topics.

- Get to know your child's friends and friends' parents.

- Make your values clear to your child by sending the repeated messages that shoplifting is stealing, and stealing is wrong.

- Keep tabs on your child by asking for communication regarding his or her whereabouts.

- The less supervision a child receives, the greater the probability that he or she may begin shoplifting, and as a parent you can use this information in making supervision decisions.

- If your child has shoplifted, assure your child you still care and help your son or daughter navigate the mixture of emotions that may arise from suffering the consequences of this crime.

- Cooperation with law enforcement allows you, as the parent, to reiterate your values about shoplifting. However, you can still treat your child with compassion and provide a support network during this painful time.

- Seek professional help if shoplifting becomes a recurring problem for your son or daughter.

ACTION STEPS

More "What If" questions...

Use this list of hypothetical situations to initiate a conversation about shoplifting with your child. This is a great way to discuss this topic in a non-threatening way where your child can feel free to express his or her opinions. As a parent, you can use their answers as a springboard for future discussions.

- What if your friend asked you to take something from a store to prove your loyalty to him/her?

- What if you bought something, and the cashier gave you too much change?

- What if you walked out of a store and later realize that you forgot to pay for one of the items?

- What if a friend gives you a gift that he or she shoplifted from a store – a gift you have really wanted for a long time?

- What if you're working at a store, and you know the other workers are shoplifting? If the manager comes to you and asks if you've noticed anything suspicious, would you tell him what you know?

OTHER TIPS FOR PARENTS: THE IMPORTANCE OF FAMILY

It is valuable to understand that the family plays a key role in its relationship to shoplifting. Several studies have documented a direct correlation between weak family structures and shoplifting and other offenses.

Events such as a death of a parent, deployment, divorce, separation, and the creation of stepfamilies can affect a child's behavior

Behavior changes result in part because the child's relationship with the parents has changed in some way. Also, with a new family dynamic, the amount of supervision a child receives may change, especially if a child transitions into a one-parent household. In two-parent households, a child tends to have lower levels of persistent shoplifting offenses. For a single parent, this information can be disheartening, especially when that parent is doing his or her best to provide for the family. With that parent's job responsibilities, it is sometimes physically and financially impossible for the parent to provide adequate adult supervision. Clearly, there comes an age where a child, if trustworthy, can be left alone for periods of time. This level of independence can be helpful for working single parents. However, too many unsupervised hours could open the door for risky behavior like shoplifting.

For younger children, parents may find themselves in a catch-22: they need to work, but the price of daycare or private babysitters can be cost-prohibitive. Sometimes parents in this situation are lucky enough to have a family member or trusted friend to care for the children. Or, parents may "trade" services to find an agreeable solution, where one parent babysits, and the other parent provides a service in exchange (free car repair, tutoring, etc.). This can be a successful arrangement if the working parent has a talent or strength in a particular area that the other parent finds valuable. Other parents may trade babysitting time. Maybe one parent works during the day, so the other parent watches the kids. Then, at night, the parents switch duties. This is especially beneficial when both families have babysitting needs that the other parent can meet.

Some families have found a way for both parents (in divorce or separation situations) to share custody of the children and adjust their work schedules around the days the children are not at home. Obviously, this is a sensitive issue and should be treated as such. When a family goes through a divorce, separation or remarriage, this is a traumatic time for all involved parties, and each family has its own unique set of circumstances. By keeping the children's emotional needs at the top of the list during this challenging time, parents will be able to help their children work through these difficulties and prevent them from engaging in harmful activities like shoplifting.

Family connections prove to protect against deviant behavior

These attachments include the strength of family unity, the depth of the parent/child relationship, the amount of time a child spends with parents, and the degree of parental supervision the child receives. Parental supervision has been discussed in the previous section, but let's take a closer look at family unity and time spent together.

Research shows that nurturing a strong, cohesive family unit is a vital element not only in a child's emotional development, but in shoplifting prevention as well. Children with weak family attachments are 50% more likely to become habitual offenders.[19] So, how do families, with work, busy schedules, and possibly more than one child balance their responsibilities and still build family unity? Trying to find ways to get involved in your child's life is key. Take a look at the following suggestions for greater involvement in your child's life:

Work to create family identity

Dr. Phil McGraw stresses the importance of the child's sense of being part of a larger whole. When the family is viewed as a team, where each person contributes to its success or failure, the child gains a sense of importance and value. With a team-oriented mindset, the parents can establish family norms and mores. It is essential to clearly articulate the family's values and help the child understand how those values apply to real-life situations. Then, if a child is breaking the family value system, parents can send the message that "Our family doesn't treat people with disrespect," or "Our family doesn't steal," etc.

---

[19] From ShopliftingIsStealing.com, p. 15

Physical proximity is important to children

Allow your child to accompany you on errands and help you with chores around the house. Even when you are doing basic housekeeping, this time can be used to work together on a project (like cleaning out the garage, doing laundry, or cooking) and gives you a chance to talk to your child and listen to him or her. Even if you're working on the computer or reading a book, your child can be in the same room with you doing something separate. The physical proximity provides an element of safety for your child and is beneficial in creating stronger family bonds. Time together driving to and from events often is a good time to talk with your child. If your child has friend(s) along, it is also a good time to learn what is going on in their lives by "eavesdropping" on their conversations. Teens often are willing to talk to you while driving at night. Darkness seems to help some of them "open up."

Quality time is important

People have heated debates about which is more important – quality time (how you spend the time with your child) or quantity of time (how many minutes and hours you spend together). All debates aside, time with your child that is focused solely on him or her – quality time – is imperative for a child in order to cultivate a sense of well-being. With parents' time being so limited, take whatever measures you can to make the time you devote to your child as meaningful as possible.

You can schedule a "date" with your child: go to a movie, grab a bite to eat, or just play a board game together. This preplanned activity will be something you and your child can look forward to, and if your child has input in the activity, he or she will probably show more excitement and commitment to the plan. During your time together, it is helpful to turn off all electronics – cell phones, televisions, etc. This makes it clear that you are focused on your child. A distracted parent who is busy texting and taking phone calls the entire time may inadvertently be sending a message to the child that "others" are more important than this one-on-one time with the child.

Besides individual time with your son or daughter, do things together as a family. Attending a sporting event, school function, or simply spending an evening together at home will build lasting memories for you and your children that also help to strengthen family ties. An added bonus of spending time together means that you have an opportunity to discuss certain issues such as drugs, alcohol, sex, and shoplifting. Use news stories as topics for discussion. When your children are accustomed to this time together as a family, they may grow more comfortable discussing touchy topics and asking you questions – questions that may prevent your children from participating in dangerous behaviors in the future. The more we as parents get involved with our children, the more we help prevent our children from making the wrong decisions. Even teenagers, who may feel they are too "cool" for family time, can be convinced to spend time with siblings and parents – you may just need to be a little more creative with this challenging age group.

> **"Use news stories as topics for discussion."**

Some parents find that if a friend is allowed to accompany the family on a day trip or outing, then the teen is more than happy to go. For other teens, just having a say in the activity itself can be a motivator. For instance, many teen girls who love to shop are excited about the prospect of spending time with the family if it means visiting their favorite stores (and possibly being able to make some purchases at those stores). If you think about your child's interests and activities, you can use this knowledge to predict which activities may be well-received by your child. It may take some trial-and-error, but if you persevere, you have an excellent chance of finding some opportunities to spend valuable time together – time that everyone enjoys!

KEY POINTS

- Traumatic events in the family, such as death of a parent, deployment, divorce, separation, and the creation of stepfamilies may make your child more susceptible to the temptation of shoplifting.

- Adequately supervising your child may be difficult when the family experiences the loss of a parent through death, divorce or separation.

- Consider creative babysitting options, such as trading babysitting for other services, adjusting work schedules, and enlisting the help of trusted friends and relatives.

- Children with weak family attachments are more likely to become involved with shoplifting.

- Families can work to create unity by building a family identity, talking about the family's values, recognizing the importance of physical proximity, and spending quality time together.

- Family identity gives a child a sense of purpose because that child feels that he or she is a contributing member to the family as a whole.

- Children enjoy being close to their parents, even when both are engaged in different activities.

- When spending time as a family, make it clear to your child that you are focused on him or her.

TIPS FOR EDUCATORS

Teachers and administrators play an important role in shoplifting prevention. School is the place where children spend the majority of their daytime hours. Legally, the role of the school is to serve in loco parentis. This means that the school officials agree to take on the role of the parents when those children are in their care. Educators can be extremely helpful in steering students away from shoplifting.

Schools Can Benefit From Teaming Up Wit Local Law Enforcement

Many schools have partnered with their local law enforcement department to improve school safety and to implement programs like D.A.R.E. (Drug Abuse Resistance Education). In many elementary schools, students have a police officer visit their classrooms regularly for these drug prevention lessons. The benefits of programs like this are two-fold: first, the children learn invaluable information about drugs, tobacco and alcohol that may or may not be discussed at home. Secondly, students get to know the police officer. (Most officers work with the classes for at least a year or two). The majo -

ity of children begin to view law enforcement officials as being a - proachable, concerned about their safety and "on their side." They come to realize that they can count on the officers to keep them safe, rather than believing the officer's sole purpose is to "catch" kids doing something wrong. By middle school, some of these police officers may be summoned to the school in a different role – if there is a fight, bullying incident, or other illegal activity that takes place on school grounds, the police will be called to intervene.

> **“Consider expanding the role of your local law enforcement to address shoplifting with children.”**

With some of these partnerships already in place, consider expanding the role of your local law enforcement to address shoplifting with children. Along with educating them about the dangers of drugs and alcohol, police officers can teach children about the risks and consequences of shoplifting. Establishing a conversation at a young age allows the police officer to repeat the message as the child advances through various grade levels. The police officer can bring a retail merchant or partner with the local Chamber of Commerce to talk to students about how shoplifting impacts stores, retail merchants and customers. For children whose parents discuss the topic of shoplifting at home, it sends a message that the school, family, retailers and community are united on the shoplifting issue. If you already have an officer who works at your school, work with him or her to find a way to introduce shoplifting prevention into that officer's existing role in the building. Many communities have found that by using the dramatic *Shoplifting IS Stealing*™ video and ancillary materials with their students, they are taking strides to inform students of the serious consequences of shoplifting and also send a strong message of prevention to young people. Using these materials is an excellent way to reinforce honesty as a core value of the school and community, too. If your school doesn't have this partnership in place, start today! Work with your local police force to improve communication and collaboration. The time the officers take to educate children equates to prevention of illegal activities. A reduced juvenile crime rate benefits the police force and the community enjoys safer neighborhoods and schools. Visit www.ShopliftingIsStealing.com for information on our resources for a Community Program.

Action Steps You Can Take

Make the most of the visit from your local law enforcement official. While sharing the facts about shoplifting and other dangerous activities is important, merely citing facts and figures isn't enough for students. To really make the connection and engage them in the lessons, be sure to plan activities that require students to use higher-level thinking skills. This critical thinking will allow the students to apply what they are learning to their own lives, and the chances that students will use this information effectively is much greater if they understand the personal connections. The following suggested activities will get you started with making the learning not only informative, but fun as well!

Role Play: What would you do if...?

This activity allows the children to practice empowering strategies to learn how to deal with peer pressure and the temptation to shoplift. This activity can be implemented in several ways:

Alternative #1: You may wish to randomly assign situations to small groups of students to act out how they would handle each situation before you teach them anything about shoplifting. This will allow you, as a presenter, to gauge the children's understanding and mindset before you begin. "Knowing your audience" is the key purpose, and the role playing situations are a wonderful springboard for discussion of similar scenarios as you introduce more information about the topic of shoplifting.

Alternative #2: After teaching students about shoplifting, ask them to use what they know to role play each scenario with solutions in which the actors do the right thing. This lets the kids think of creative solutions to issues that don't always have a single correct answer.

Alternative #3: This is similar to #2, except before having them act out the situation with a positive solution, have them try to act out the "wrong" options first. This allows them to compare and contrast the choices. Educational research has found that when students use classification skills like comparing and contrasting information, the learning experience is enhanced.

"What Would You Do If...?" Scenarios:

Directions to Students: Act out the following situation. Based on the directions you have been given, decide how the characters in each situation choose to respond to their circumstances.

• Gang initiation. (Situation: Nick wants to be part of a gang and is told by the gang leader that a rite of passage is to shoplift sneakers and a jacket from a popular retail store. They walk into the store, and the gang leader spots the shoes and coat. He points them out to Nick, saying, "I'll wait for you outside. Don't bother coming out unless you've got the shoes and jacket with you.")

- Pressure to fit into the "in" group. (Situation: Sally wants to bcome friends with a certain group of kids, and she learns that this group likes to shoplift for fun. When she meets up with them at the mall on Friday night, she is excited to find out they finally want he to hang out with them. They walk into a beauty supply store, and, one by one, each girl grabs an item and shoves it in her purse – nail polish, lip gloss, etc. Marci, one of the girls from the group, says, "Sally, what do you want? Take your pick! C'mon, it's no big deal.")

- Child tries to get attention. (John's parents never seem to have time for him. His dad works nights, so he's asleep whenever John's awake. His mother works at a restaurant, which means she gets to see John for less than ten minutes a day before it's time for her to report to work each evening. One night, John and his friend, Dan, walk to the local convenience store. John has the money to pay for his sad excuse for a "dinner," but can't believe that he has to use his money to feed himself. "Why can't my mom cook a meal for me like everyone else's mom does?" he grumbles to his friend. Dan responds, "So why pay? A hot dog costs this store next to nothing. You shouldn't have to waste your money because your parents don't take the time to feed you...")

- Girl really wants new jeans, but she can't afford them. (Situation: Brianne walks into the boutique to look at the cute jeans she's been eyeing for weeks. She checks the tag: $98. Brielle digs through her purse, but she knows the $25 from babysitting won't even begin to cover the jeans. Just for fun, she tries them on. They fit perfectly, and they even match what she's wearing! Brielle peeks out of the dressing room. The only clerk on duty is busy with a demanding customer and her whining toddler. With no metal detector in sight, Brianne is positive the clerk won't notice if she walks out the door, wearing the jeans...)

• Girlfriend/boyfriend's birthday – can't afford gift. (Situation: Mark's girlfriend showed him a necklace she liked. With her birthday coming up, he would love to buy it for her. Unfortunately, he doesn't have enough money saved up. Mark's best friend works at the store selling the necklace and offers to "take care of it" for Mark, as long as Mark gives him $50. The necklace is more than double that price, and Mark knows his friend is not paying for the necklace.)

Game: Four Corners

This is a great way to associate the dangers of shoplifting with that of drugs, alcohol, and tobacco. Put four signs in each corner of the room (Signs: #1: Shoplifting; #2: Drugs; #3: Alcohol; #4: Tobacco). One student leaves the room (or closes his/her eyes). The other students choose a corner to stand in. Once students have chosen their corners, the student who is "it" calls out one of the four categories. That same student must then give a fact that he or she has been learning about that topic.

If the student is correct, all children standing in that corner are "out" and return to their desks. Explain to students that this means they are now "out of jail." The students remaining in the corners have not yet been "bailed out" and continue choosing corners! After the first round, a new person is designated to be "it", the remaining students choose a corner again, and the game continues the same way ("It" chooses a topic and states a fact, which –if correct – students in that corner are now "out"). Play continues until only one student is left, and that person (still considered to be "in jail") has the opportunity to get "out" by stating a correct fact. In this game, everyone with knowledge of the facts has the chance to be a winner.

Shoplifting Attitudes Survey

Give your students this assessment as a before and after measure to get to know students' attitudes and knowledge of shoplifting. When used as a post-test, you can compare the answers from the pre-test to look for growth and new understandings.

Make it clear to the students that you want their honest opinions and will not count this against them. You might also have to have a conversation about "snitching or ratting." Tell them this assessment has no impact on anyone. Instead, you merely want to use it as a means of initiating a dialogue about shoplifting. Administering this anonymously is another way to elicit honest responses.

Rate the following on a scale from 1 to 5:
1= Strongly Disagree
2= Somewhat Disagree
3= Neutral/No Opinion
4= Somewhat Agree
5= Strongly Agree

- Shoplifting is a serious crime.

- Many students in my school shoplift.

- Taking school supplies (pencils, paper, etc.) home to keep without asking is okay to do.

- Taking something from the lost and found that isn't mine (but hasn't been claimed) is okay.

• Shoplifting is an important topic to learn about in school.

• If I'm with a friend while he or she stole something from a store, it is wrong for both of us to get in trouble with the police.

• Stealing something small, like a candy bar or makeup, is no big deal.

• If my little brother or sister takes a pack of gum out of the store, it's not really shoplifting.

• It's okay if I don't pay for something at the store if the clerk forgot to charge me for it.

• If the cashier at the mall gives me too much change accidentally, it's not considered shoplifting.

• It's okay to eat some food at the store (grapes, loose candy in a bin) without paying for it if I want to see if it's good, fresh, etc.

Promoting a Positive School Atmosphere

Dedicated educators are concerned not only with a student's academic progress but also with his or her social and emotional development. As many parents and teachers know, educators can and do make a difference in children's lives, and sometimes the most profound impact is made when teachers, counselors, and administrators help children through difficult times in their lives. Family problems, violence in the community, and friendship problems are all very real concerns that today's students face. The caring teachers who positively influence a child or set a learning environment in the classroom that is safe allows a child (who may be headed down the wrong path) to thrive. By making school a protected, nurturing place for children and teens, educators can do their part to prevent shoplifting and other crimes.

School climate committees (e.g., committees that focus on improving the atmosphere in the building and create programs/activities to promote a positive school climate) can coordinate efforts to promote a team mentality among students and staff. Students and teachers in a school where everyone works towards common, positive goals sense they are part of a larger "team," and just as the family unit has its own norms, the school can promote its values and expectations for students and staff. Students in this type of school are inundated with the message that "This is how we act at our school," or "We just don't do x at our school," etc. With teacher and student buy-in, we can help students develop the confidence and conviction to lead responsible lives and resist participation in illegal activities like shoplifting.

Giving attention and recognition to students who are excellent role models is another great way to highlight desired behaviors and personality traits. Some schools nominate "Star Students," "Student Leaders," or "Student Legends." The name does not matter, but the message is the same –good citizenship has its own intrinsic and extrinsic rewards. This can be a motivating element in a child's mind. When students see that it's not just the "bad" kids who get attention from teachers (even if it's negative attention) or outstanding athletes who are honored, they will be more inclined to make better choices.

Character education is another tool that schools are using to make positive strides with their students. In one New Jersey school, teachers use their homeroom period (known as "advisory") each day to teach character-building lessons about bullying, goal-setting, friendships, and more. This particular school structures this period so that each teacher has a very small group of students (no more than fifteen) to advise. This way, the teacher has the entire school year to establish strong rapport with those students and to serve as a mentor on real life experiences as well as academics.

Shoplifting lessons are a perfect topic for teachers to introduce during a homeroom/advisory period. These lessons would give students the time to discuss the crime itself, consequences of shoplifting, and ask a trusted adult any questions they have. In turn, the teacher can clear up misconceptions and reiterate the message that "Shoplifting IS Stealing™" and that stealing is wrong and has its own set of consequences for those who choose to steal.

> **" *Shoplifting lessons are a perfect topic for teachers to introduce during a homeroom/advisory period.* "**

In addition to these activities, teachers, guidance counselors, coaches and other trusted adults can assist students in better decision-making skills. When students have trusted adults they can rely on, they can go to that person confidentially and share any issues they may have in their lives. The counselor, teacher or coach can then be sure that the child has the tools and skills to navigate difficult situations like schoolwork difficulties, family problems, an more. And, if the adult doesn't feel qualified to address the child's issue (for example, substance abuse), that person can use the resources available in the school (or in the community) to connect the child with the appropriate people. If the school has a guidance counselor who can intervene and address the problems early, it can prevent the child from making poor choices at a later point, especially with regard to shoplifting and other illegal activities.

Programs that promote tolerance, empowerment, and confidence can have a significant impact on a student's psyche. Some schools host assemblies and organize clubs that promote pro-social behavior. One such example of this is Rachel's Challenge.

Action Steps You Can Take

Rachel's Challenge is a school-wide assembly that shares with the audience the life story of Rachel Joy Scott, one of the vibrant teenagers whose life was taken far too soon in the tragedy at Columbine High School. Rachel was the first casualty of this mass shooing, but her legacy lives on, thanks to her family and friends. After her passing, numerous classmates called the family, sharing with them acts of kindness that Rachel did for them in making them feel better, and in one instance, preventing a student from committing suicide – all because of the compassionate words from Rachel, who, during her short seventeen years, knew she could make a difference in the world.

The diary entries and other writings from Rachel were consistent with her personality: she wrote about the need for us to stand up for what's right, be unique, and leave our unique imprints on the world. Even though Rachel is not here today to witness her legacy, the Rachel's Challenge program allows schools to set up their own Rachel's Club. Students and teachers who take part in this organization work to promote a positive school climate and encourage children to be "upstanders," especially in bullying situations.

With programs like Rachel's Challenge, schools can be the positive beacons of hope that will allow children to find like-minded classmates who want to make a positive contribution in the world. By putting these kinds of programs and clubs in place, students have ready-made organizations that will lead them in the right direction and give them that all-important sense of belonging to something greater than themselves. When students feel they are an integral part of an organization (and that their contributions make a difference), they are less likely to feel lonesome, bored, or tempted to fill any voids in their lives with activities like shoplifting

After-School Supervision

In response to the high percentage of working parents, many schools offer safe, affordable daycare right in the school to be sure that all children have access to supervision before parents get home from work. During this time, trained caregivers provide students with snacks, homework help, and the opportunity to unwind by playing indoors or outside. Parents can have greater peace of mind, knowing that their sons and daughters are being supervised until they can pick them up at the end of the workday.

As students enter middle school (and move into high school), some of these services come to an end. However, many middle and high schools offer a variety of after-school activities to entice students to get involved in the extra-curricular life of the school. Some schools even offer late busses to transport students home, so that children who would not normally be able to get a ride have the opportunity to participate. Here's a short list of some of the activities offered in today's middle and high schools: dances, homework clubs, tutoring, big brothers/big sisters programs, sports, and extra-curriculars like drama, technology, art, newspaper, yearbook, etc.

Encourage After-School Activities:

Encouraging children to stay busy in the after-school hours is a great step in shoplifting prevention, as most risk-taking behaviors happen with older children and teens between the hours of 4:00 - 6:00 p.m. (when many parents are still at work and the children are unsupervised). Be attuned to your students' interests, talents, and abilities. Use this knowledge to help them find appropriate after school activities that they can get involved in. If you find there is a student who has interests that you can't find a good "match" for, you may be able to find community activities or, if you're willing, start your own club at the school to provide a safe place for children with interests that fall outside the scope of the other programs that are offered.

KEY POINTS

- Teachers and administrators play a key role in shoplifting prevention.

- Schools can effectively use law enforcement by creating partnerships between the school, the local police force, and the Chamber of Commerce.

- In addition to teaching drug and alcohol awareness, police officers can visit schools to raise awareness about shoplifting.

- Role plays, attitudinal surveys, and games are excellent ways to engage children in the topic of shoplifting and to allow them to apply their knowledge to hypothetical shoplifting situations.

- Schools that build a positive school climate influence students who may be inclined to shoplift to make better choices due to the nurturing school environment.

- School climate committees, recognition of "star students," character education, advisory periods, and involved guidance counselors can help prevent shoplifting among students by encouraging healthy, pro-social behaviors.

- After school programs can assist parents in supervising children until they get home from work.

- Extra-curricular sports and clubs provide outlets for students to establish healthy relationships and connections with others, which can be a deterrent to shoplifting temptations.

HOW TO GET YOUR COMMUNITY INVOLVED

In each community, young people are surrounded by people who form a "Circle of Influence." This includes law enforcement professionals, retail merchants, chambers of commerce, loss prevention professionals, business owners, educators, faith-based groups, youth organizations, service clubs, , and of course, family and friends. If one segment of the "Circle" teaches the legal and social consequences of shoplifting while another segment ignores the offense, our young people are receiving mixed messages. They may begin to believe that stealing is OK. Is that the message we want to deliver?

As a member of the "Circle of Influence" within your community you have many opportunities to impact young people. There are numerous ways you can make a positive difference in a child's life. The following ideas and activities will provide you with some options from which to choose.

Research shows that the integrated efforts of parents, law enforcement professionals, educators, retailers, faith community, families, friends and honest consumers play an important role in shoplifting prevention. Even taking one small step today can contribute greatly to the prevention of shoplifting. If everyone does their part – no matter how big or small – together, we can help our children understand that Shoplifting IS Stealing™.

> **"There are numerous ways you can make a positive difference in a child's life."**

Action Steps

Create a Community Awareness Task Force

Conducting a successful awareness campaign is a team effort, as shoplifting impacts the entire community. By creating a community-wide task force comprised of individuals who can collaborate and coordinate efforts, your community can raise awareness regarding shoplifting and teach children the consequences for this crime. Include the following stake-holders in this group: law enforcement, retail merchants, educators, parents, legislators (at the city and county levels), media, faith-based organizations, youth organizations, and community groups.

Launch A *Shoplifting IS Stealing!*™ Awareness Campaign

To create awareness in your community about shoplifting and its impact, conduct a community-wide *Shoplifting IS Stealing!*™Awareness Campaign.

Holding a kickoff event is a great way to generate interest and media coverage of the issue. Some communities have designated their communities "Shoplifing-Free Zones," similar to "Drug-Free Zones" near schools. Other ideas include:

- Hold a special meeting for community members to explain the program and seek endorsement,

- Post signs in store windows to alert possible shoplifters that these stores have a "zero-tolerance" policy for shoplifting,

- Distribute anti-shoplifting buttons for community members to wear,

• Have flyers with shoplifting facts available on merchants' counters to inform customers of the campaign and educate them about shoplifting.

Presenting Shoplifting Information

When planning a presentation about shoplifting, be sure to consider the age group, their needs and wants, and organize the activities and information accordingly. For example, if you decide to present shoplifting information to business merchants, tailor your facts and figures to statistics that apply to businesses. Provide tips and assistance that will curtail shoplifting in their stores and help their businesses grow. If the audience understands there is a payoff for them to take part in this *Shoplifting IS Stealing!*™ *Community Awareness Campaign,* you are much more likely to receive their support and commitment.

Use the *Shoplifting IS Stealing*™ *Community Awareness Campaign* materials to plan your programming. The materials in the program contain information you will need to present programs to families, merchants, faith-based organizations, etc. See the "Resources" section for more details.

Involve Children

Run a *Shoplifting IS Stealing*™ poster contest in your community's schools. This will reinforce your campaign and raise awareness among children. You can then post winning entries in highly-visible community locations (stores, public library, etc.). If you offer prizes for the winning posters, you will find that you have many willing children ready to share their artistic talents with the community!

Publicize Your Events

Spreading the word about the *Shoplifting IS Stealing!*™ *Community Awareness Campaign* and any other events you have planned to help children make good decisions about shoplifting takes commitment. Ask community leaders and retail merchants for their support. Do short presentations at schools, at community organizations, and in other venues where family and children are likely to hear the message and become involved.

Send out copies of the event announcement in online and offline publications of schools, chambers of commerce, faith organizations, youth groups and post these copies in public places. Depending on the size of event and expected audience, a "Save the date" card or invitation should be sent out four to six weeks prior to the event. In the schools, you could give students bookmarks or other giveaways to explain and advertise the event.

Contact local television and radio stations. Ask about their policies for running public service announcements (PSAs) on shoplifting. Depending on the event size, be sure to call several weeks in advance to ensure you submit the appropriate information in time. Get familiar with local newspapers, and magazines. Is there a regular column that targets youth, or perhaps local interest stories? Contact that reporter and pitch your ideas to him or her.

Obtain a calendar of trade shows or expos to share the *Shoplifting IS Stealing!*™ program with the public. You might even consider county or state fairs as a place to let the public know about the program. There are often booths or areas for organizations to display their materials.

Remember to follow-up. After your event is covered by the local media, has appeared in a story, or has been broadcast, send the reporter a thank you note. It doesn't take much time to do this, and your courtesy will be remembered by that person. To preview the contents of the Community Awareness Campaign visit www.ShopliftingIsStealing.com.

KEY POINTS

- Communities can use their "Circle of Influence" to raise shoplifting awareness.

- This "Circle of Influence" can include community members such as the police, chambers of commerce, schools, faith-based groups, retail merchants, youth clubs, service organizations, etc.

- Communities can create task forces to launch a *Shoplifting IS Stealing!™ Community Awareness Campaign* to raise community awareness about shoplifting.

- An effective way to launch this campaign is by holding a high-profile, exciting kick-off event

- The task force can plan presentations to share with merchants, law enforcement, schools, and more.

- Programs should be tailored to meet the needs and interests of each target group.

- *Shoplifting IS Stealing*™ materials can help your group run an effective shoplifting awareness campaign.

- Be sure to publicize any campaign events to increase awareness further.

ADDITIONAL RESOURCES

Shoplifting IS Stealing! ™ offers a wide variety of programs, activities and resources to help all members of the community to work together to prevent shoplifting. The following resources are available at www.ShopliftingIsStealing.com.

The Shoplifting IS Stealing! ™ book

This book deepens your understanding of shoplifting and offers tools, ideas and resources to help you prevent kids from becoming involved with it. The *Shoplifting IS Stealing!* ™ book is an ideal resource for parents, teachers, law enforcement professionals, social service professionals, faith leaders, business owners or community leaders who want to help kids make better decisions and avoid starting down the path of juvenile crime. It features the following:

- Shoplifting facts and statistics

- Reasons why people – especially children – shoplift

- The costs and consequences of shoplifting

- Signs that your child may be shoplifting

- Tips on how to prevent children from shoplifting – ideal for parents, educators, and community leaders

- Links to online shoplifting resources and more!

Shoplifting IS Stealing! ™ DVD with discussion guide

This hard-hitting video can be used in a number of ways throughout the community. Especially effective is its use as a gift to local schools and public libraries---donated by businesses, service clubs or individuals. It is designed to be viewed by kids ages 8-18+. It is ideal to have an adult guide have an interactive conversation about shoplifting using the companion Discussion Guide. (Downloadable with purchase.)

Through the story of Brian, a 17-year-old convicted shoplifter who looks back on when he first started shoplifting "just for fun" at age 12, this impactful video addresses the emotional, criminal, and economic consequences of shoplifting.

Kids learn that shoplifting is not a game and how it can negatively impact their lives, their families as well as the communities they live in.

Community Awareness Package: This includes the following products and support materials to help you convey the message that "Shoplifting IS Stealing" to children and others in your community.

• *Shoplifting IS Stealing!*™ Book

• *Shoplifting IS Stealing!* ™ DVD and Discussion Guide

• *Shoplifting IS Stealing!*™ Community Awareness Handbook which includes:
- 52 pages of presentation tips, activities, sample press releases, publicity ideas and list of resources.
- Multiple user license for up to five users of the material
- Discussion Guide and Terminology
- Shoplifting Facts and Statistics Report

Visit www.ShopliftingIsStealing.com to view the Awareness Handbook's Table of Contents.

Posters: A series of three uniquely designed posters, each with a different message to attract the attention of the consumer.

Buttons: Coordinated with each poster, the buttons are for employees to wear to remind the public about the campaign.

Message Cards: These cards can be placed in customers' packages, distributed to schools, placed on business counters and in other public places. The front of the card carries the same design as the poster. The back features information on the costs and impact of shoplifting on the honest consumer, thus building support for the merchants' efforts to apprehend shoplifters.

Stickers: These stickers coordinate with the designs on the poster. They will adhere to store shelving to warn customers that in this store shoplifting is prosecuted

Pencils: White pencils with the red message *Shoplifting IS Stealing!* ™ can be given to students during classroom presentations.

For more information, to request order forms or order products visit www.ShopliftingIsStealing.com

ABOUT THE AUTHOR

Judy Whalen is the founder of the *Shoplifting IS Stealing!* ™ program and is passionate about making a difference in the world we live in. She originally created the *Shoplifting IS Stealing!*™ prevention program to help parents, teachers and community members across the U.S. work together to raise awareness about shoplifting and provide them with effective strategies to prevent kids from becoming shoplifters. For over 15 years this program has been successfully used by numerous communities and tens of thousands of adults who want to help kids make the wise decisions.

Judy is also the CEO and founder of *It Starts With Us, Inc.*™ which is a family of programs and services to help individuals, families and organizations communicate effectively and design their lives and business around their core values. In addition to *Shoplifting IS Stealing!* ™ these entities include: Center for Strategic Change,LLC ™ and Strengthen the Harmony between Your Life Family & Work ™.

As a highly sought after management consultant, she has guided numerous boards of directors of organizations through a variety of strategic thinking activities; coached CEO's, leadership teams and individuals; conducted board and staff retreats, and presented on various topics at state, regional and national conferences and created the programs mentioned above. Judy's clients include school districts, health care organizations, day care centers, large international trade associations, nonprofits of all shapes and sizes and private corporations and individuals.

Judy has a Bachelor of Science degree in education from the University of Wisconsin-Whitewater. In addition, she has graduate credits in public policy and has completed the six-year Institute for Organization Management at Notre Dame, sponsored by the U.S. Chamber of Commerce. She currently chairs the Dean's Advisory Board for the College of Education and Professional Studies at University of Wisconsin-Whitewater. She is also a current Board member of the Dane County Council of Public Affairs.

Contact Information:
Judy Whalen
Judy@ShopliftingIsStealing.com
www.ShopliftingIsStealing.com
facebook.com/ShopliftingIsStealing

www.ingramcontent.com/pod-product-compliance
Lightning Source LLC
Chambersburg PA
CBHW071730090426
42738CB00011B/2444